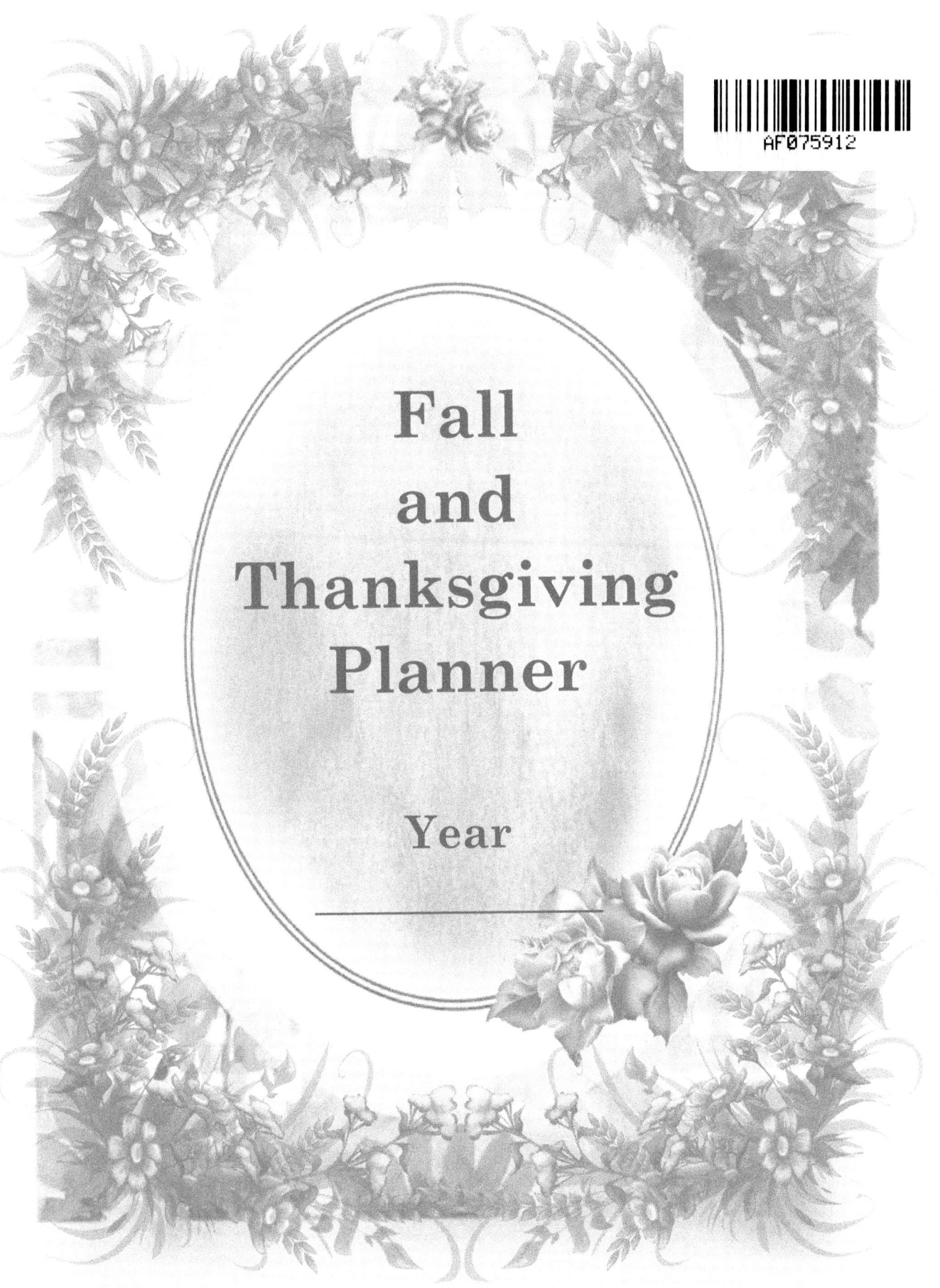

People I am Thankful for

Name	What they mean to me

Things I am Grateful for

1.
2.
3.
4.
5.
6.
7.
8.
9.
10.
11.
12.
13.
14.
15.
16.
17.
18.
19.
20.

Daily Gratitude

Daily Gratitude

1.
2.
3.
4.
5.
6.
7.
8.
9.
10.
11.
12.
13.
14.
15.
16.
17.
18.
19.
20.
21.
22.
23.
24.
25.
26.
27.
28.
29.
30.
31.

Favorite Fall and Thanksgiving Quotes

Favorite Fall and Thanksgiving Quotes

Favorite Fall and Thanksgiving Quotes

Thanksgiving Planning Calendar

October

MON	TUES	WED	THURS	FRI	SAT	SUN
☐	☐	☐	☐	☐	☐	☐
☐	☐	☐	☐	☐	☐	☐
☐	☐	☐	☐	☐	☐	☐
☐	☐	☐	☐	☐	☐	☐
☐	☐	☐	☐	☐	☐	☐

NOTES

Thanksgiving Planning Calendar

November

MON	TUES	WED	THURS	FRI	SAT	SUN
☐	☐	☐	☐	☐	☐	☐
☐	☐	☐	☐	☐	☐	☐
☐	☐	☐	☐	☐	☐	☐
☐	☐	☐	☐	☐	☐	☐
☐	☐	☐	☐	☐	☐	☐

NOTES

Weekly Planner

Tasks

- Monday
- Tuesday
- Wednesday
- Thursday

Week of

Shopping List

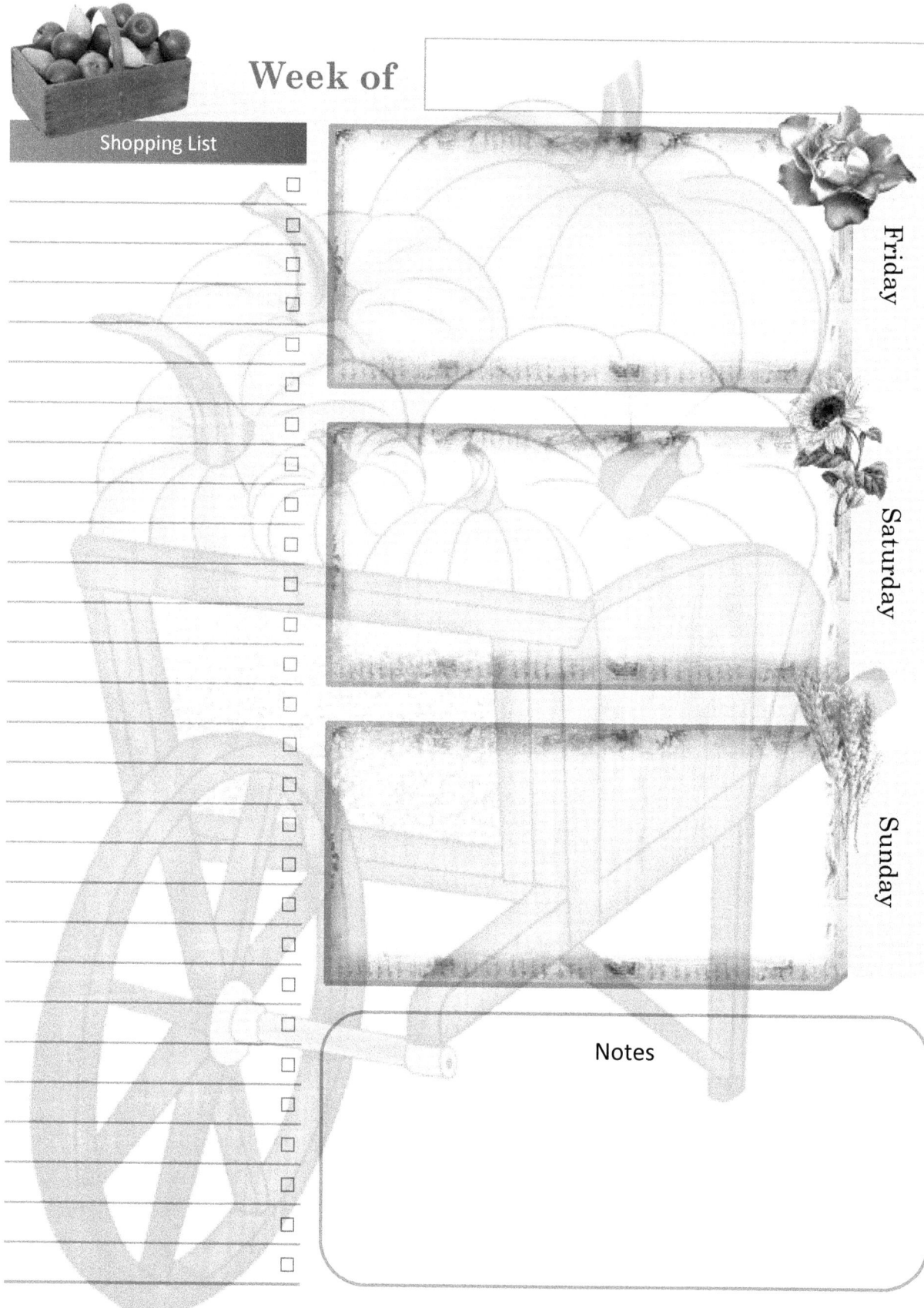

Friday

Saturday

Sunday

Notes

Budget

Month

Item	Budget	Actual
Regular Monthly Expenses		
Food		
Refreshments		
Décor		
Table Decor		
Outings		
Thanksgiving Cards		
Thanksgiving DIY Gifts and Crafts		
Entertainment		

Fall Weekly Exercise Plan

	Warm Up	Workout	Duration	Notes
Mon				
Tues				
Wed				
Thurs				
Fri				
Sat				
Sun				

Weekly Yard Work Schedule

	Task	How Often	Person Responsible	Notes
Mon				
Tues				
Wed				
Thurs				
Fri				
Sat				
Sun				

Fall Activity Ideas

Activity	Adults	Kids	All Ages	Notes

Places to Visit During Fall

Place	Cost	Notes

Color-Fall Scenic Trips

Destination	Route	Walk	Cycle	Car	Train	Notes

Planning Notes

Recipe Index

Recipe	Source	Make Ahead

Recipe for

Ingredients	Method

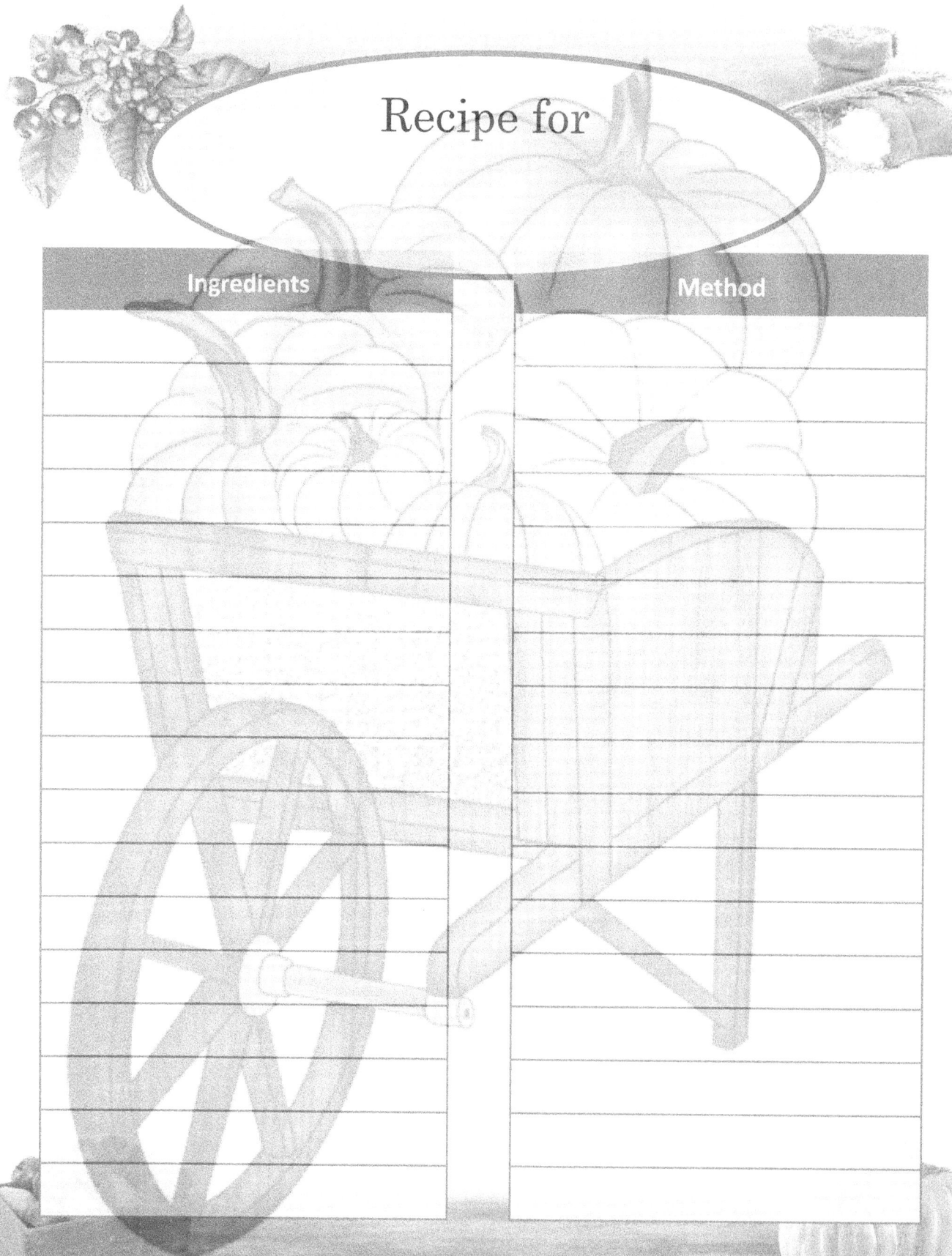

Cooking and Baking Notes

Celebrating Thanksgiving

Our Thanksgiving Traditions

Tradition	Who started it
	When it began

Tradition	Who started it
	When it began

Tradition	Who started it
	When it began

Creating New Traditions

For the Adults	For the Children

Thanksgiving Decorations

Decorations Inventory	✓	Decorations Shopping List	✓

Thanksgiving Decorations Plan

- Outside
- Door & Entrance
- Living Room
- Stairs
- Bathrooms
- Kitchen
- Thanksgiving Table
- Dining Room

Thanksgiving Dinner – Dining Out

Host:	
Venue:	
Time:	
RSVP'd	

To Take

Menu

Preparations	✓
Gifts for hosts	
Drinks	
Thanksgiving Dinner Contributions	

Thanksgiving Invitation List

Name	Address	Sent	RSVP'd

Thanksgiving Guest List

Total Guests

Name	RSVP'd	Special Requests	Bringing

Thanksgiving Dinner

Starter

Main

Dessert

Snacks and Drinks

Family & Guests at the Table	Adults	Children

Thanksgiving Menu

	Who's Bringing	To Buy	✓
STARTERS			
TURKEY			
SIDES			
DESSERT			
DRINKS			

Thanksgiving Shopping List

Dairy	✓

Produce	✓

Meat	✓

Canned	✓

Baking	✓

Other	✓

Thanksgiving Wednesday Prep

To Do	✓

To Cook	✓

Notes

Thanksgiving Dinner Cooking Schedule

Date

Time		To Do	✓
5:00 AM			
6:00 AM			
7:00 AM			
8:00 AM			
9:00 AM			
10:00 AM			
11:00 AM			
12:00 PM			
1:00 PM			
2:00 PM			
3:00 PM			
4:00 PM			
5:00 PM			
6:00 PM			
7:00 PM			
8:00 PM			
9:00 PM			

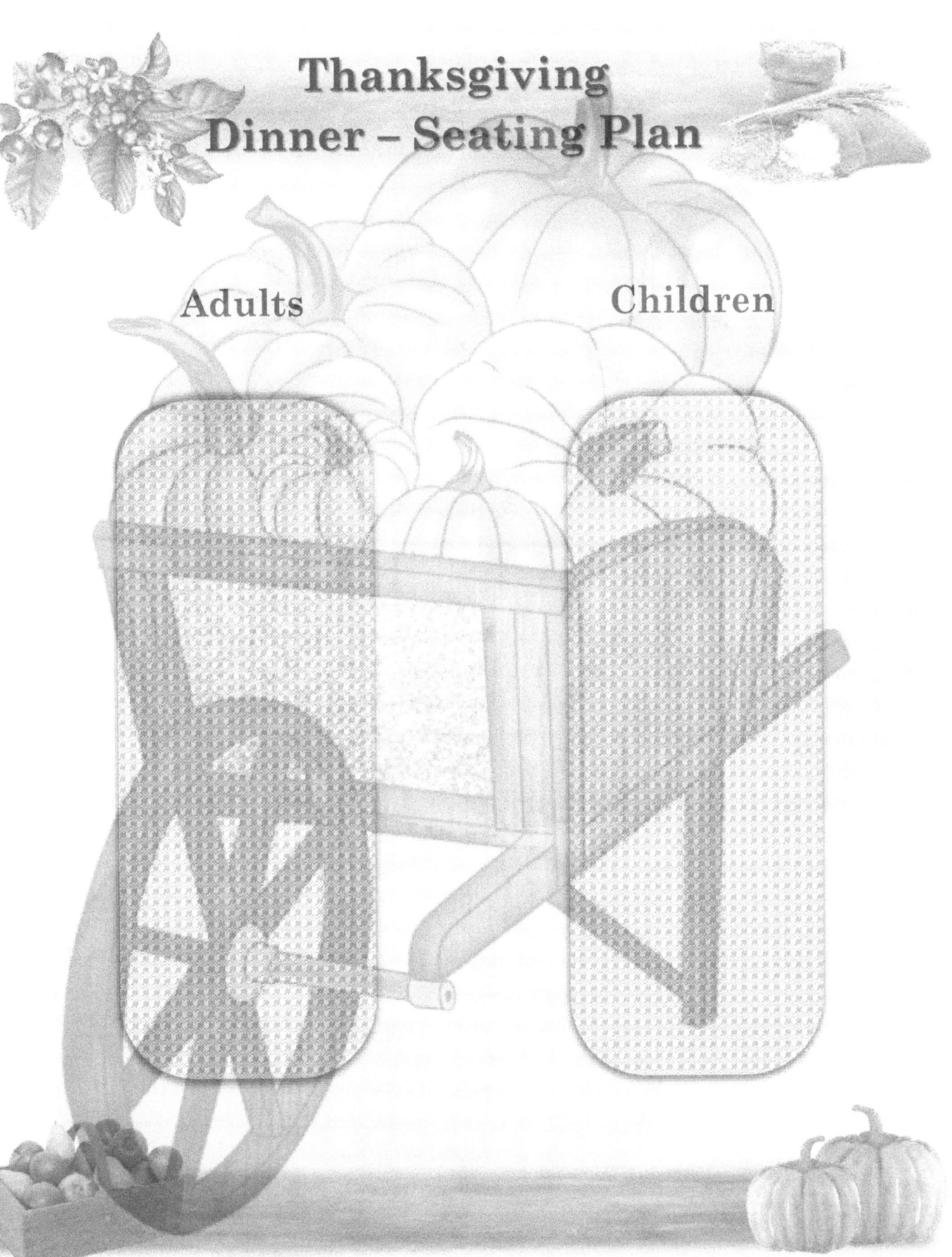

Thanksgiving Dinner

Seating Plan

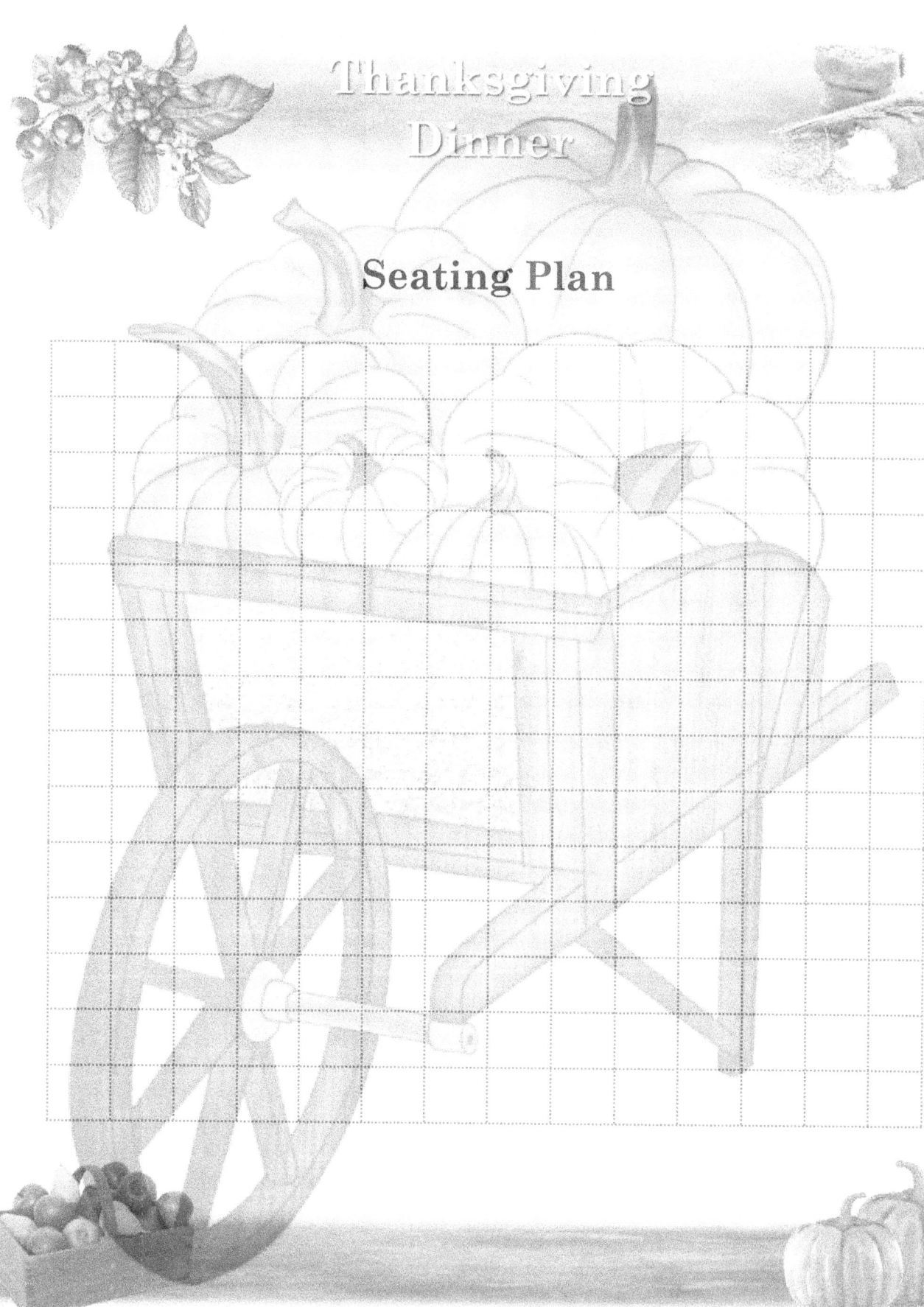

Gifts Received

Name	Gift	"Thank you" sent

Using Leftovers

Idea	Recipe Source	Notes

Black Friday Wish List

Item	Where Available	Cost

Name:

I am grateful for:

Name:

I am grateful for:

Name:

I am grateful for:

Name:

I am grateful for:

Name:

I am grateful for:

Name:

I am grateful for:

Name:

I am grateful for:

Name:

I am grateful for:

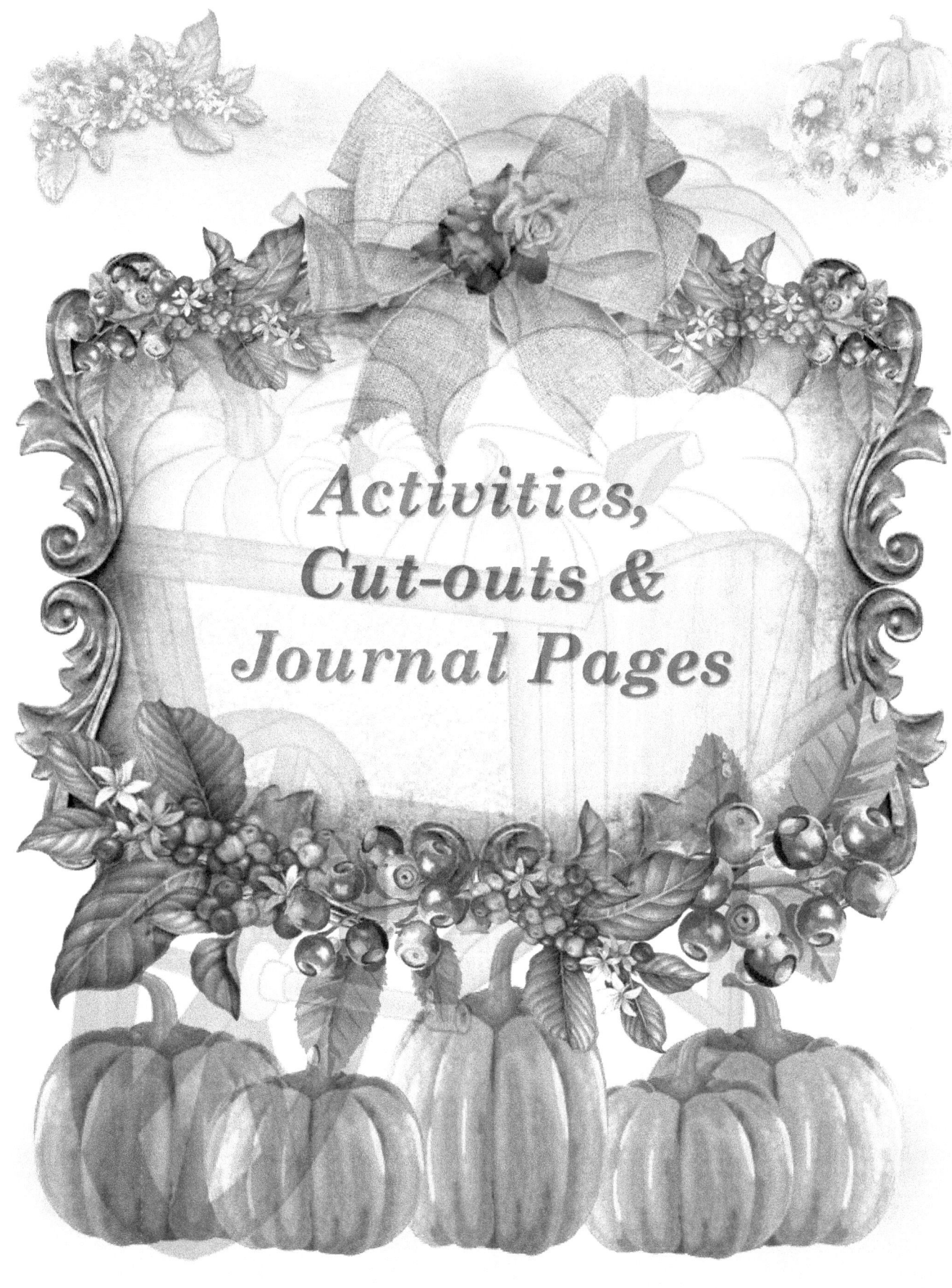

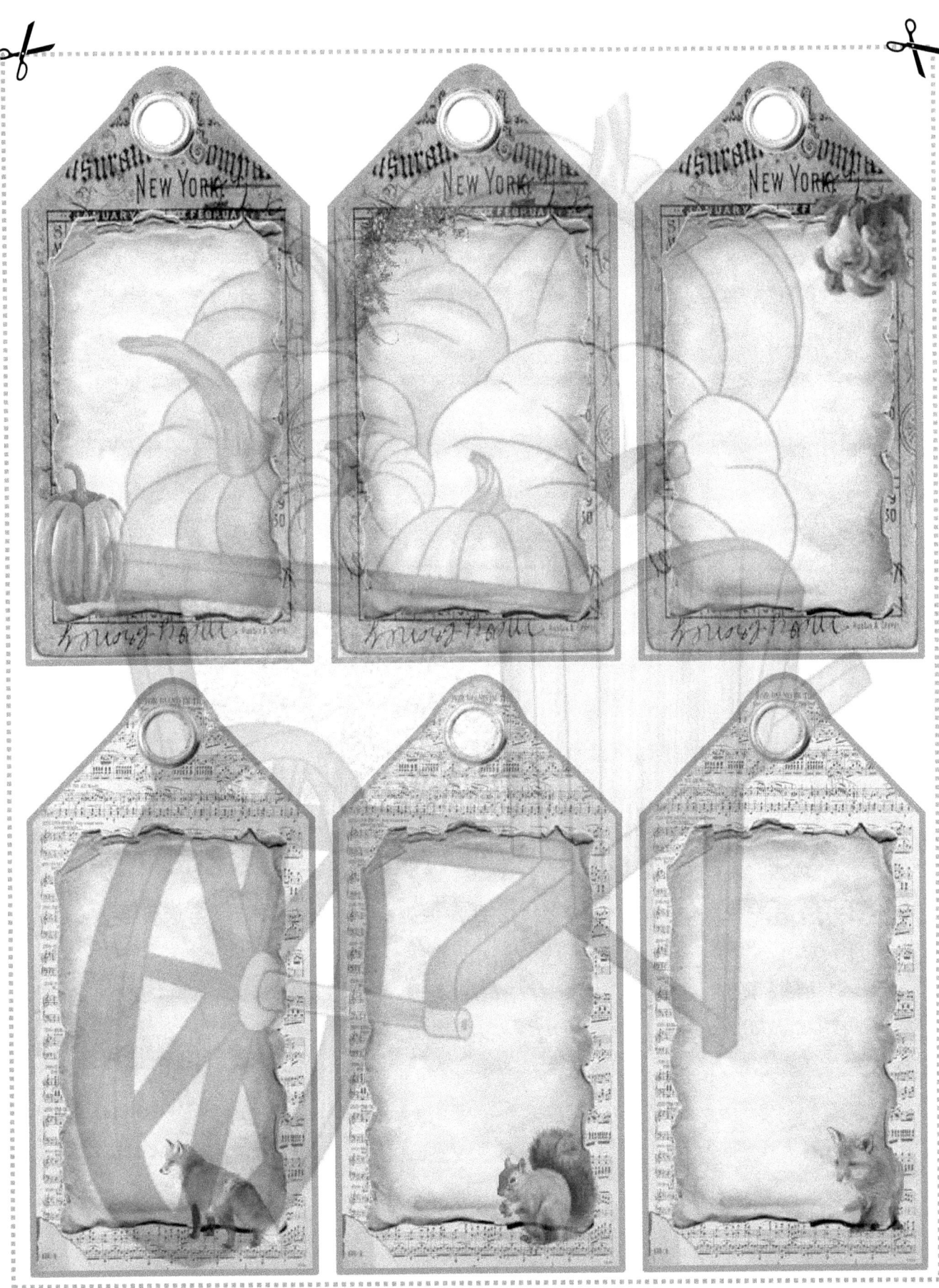

Conversation Starters

What is your Favorite Thanksgiving Food?

I am thankful for...

My favorite thing about Thanksgiving is...

What are you grateful for about the person on your Left?

The Thanksgiving tradition I enjoy the most is...

My favorite Thanksgiving family tradition is...

Count Your Blessings

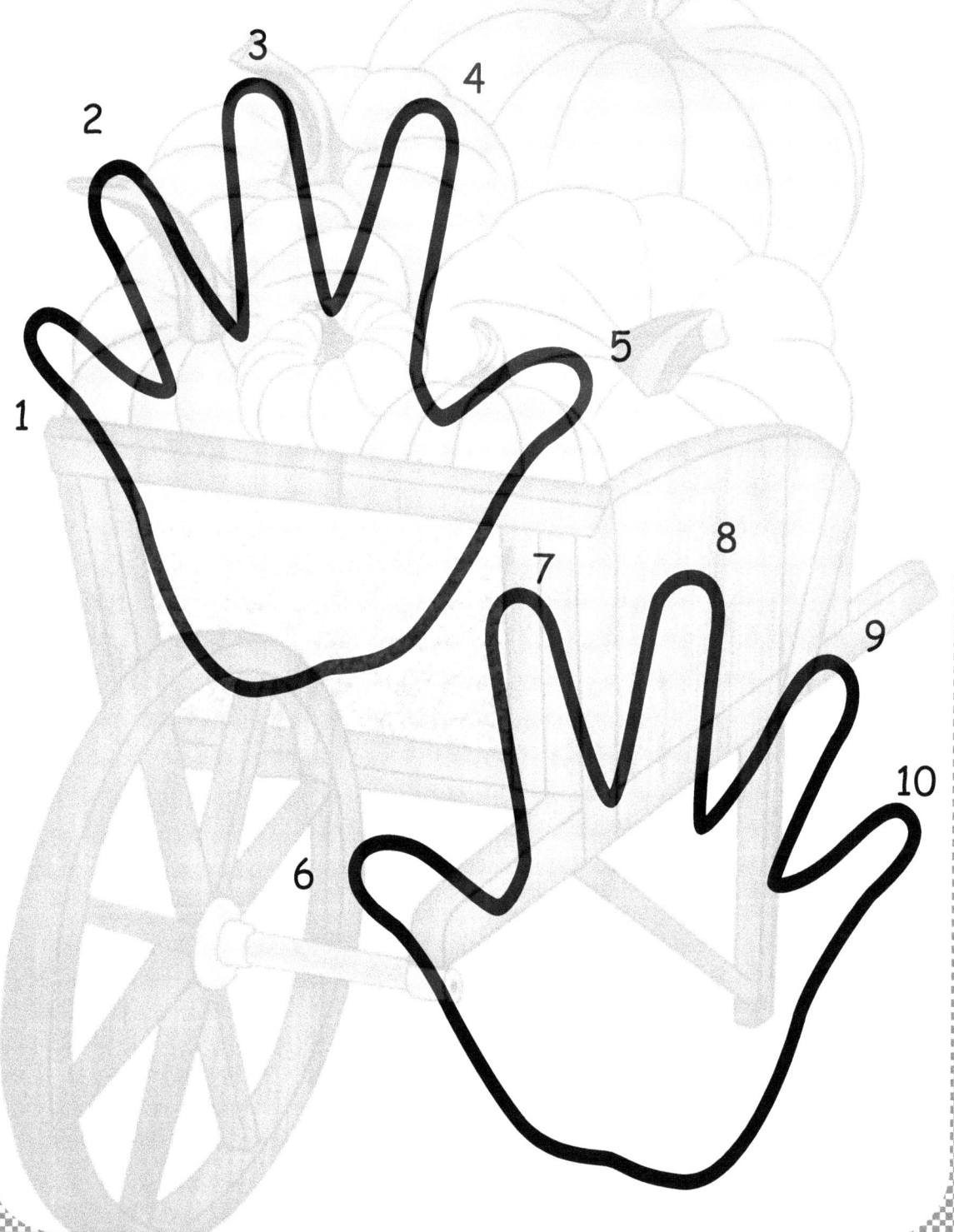

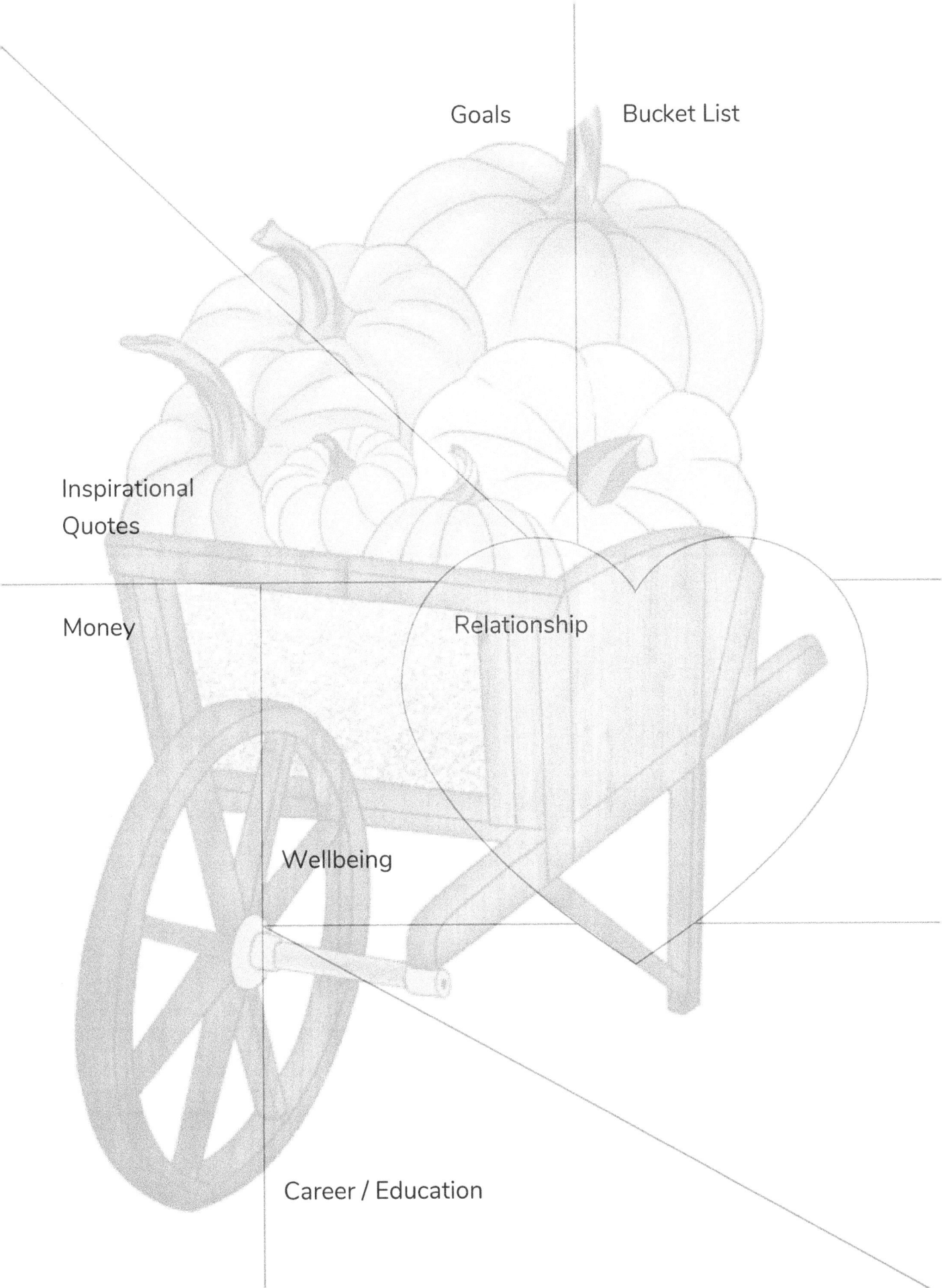

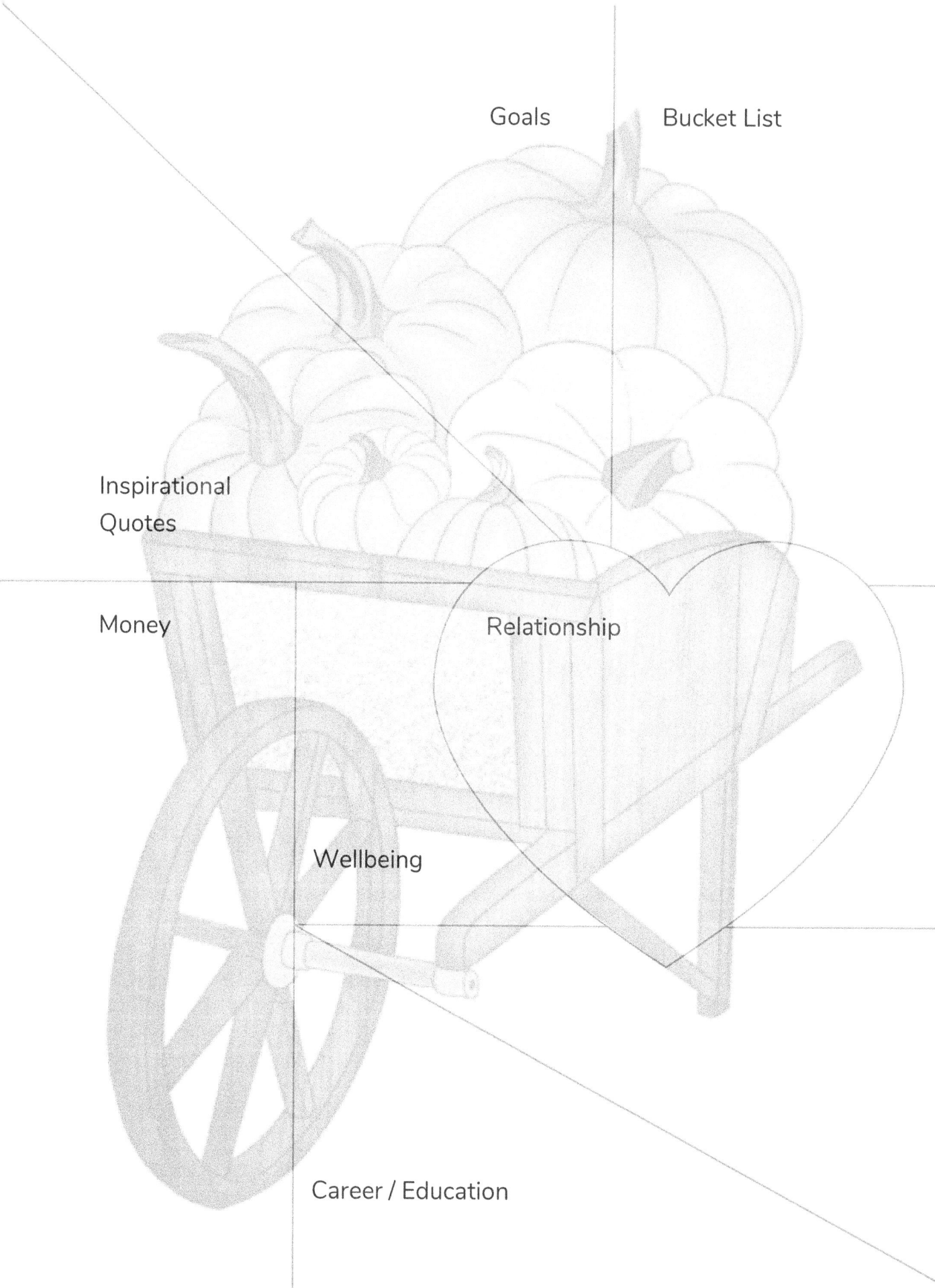

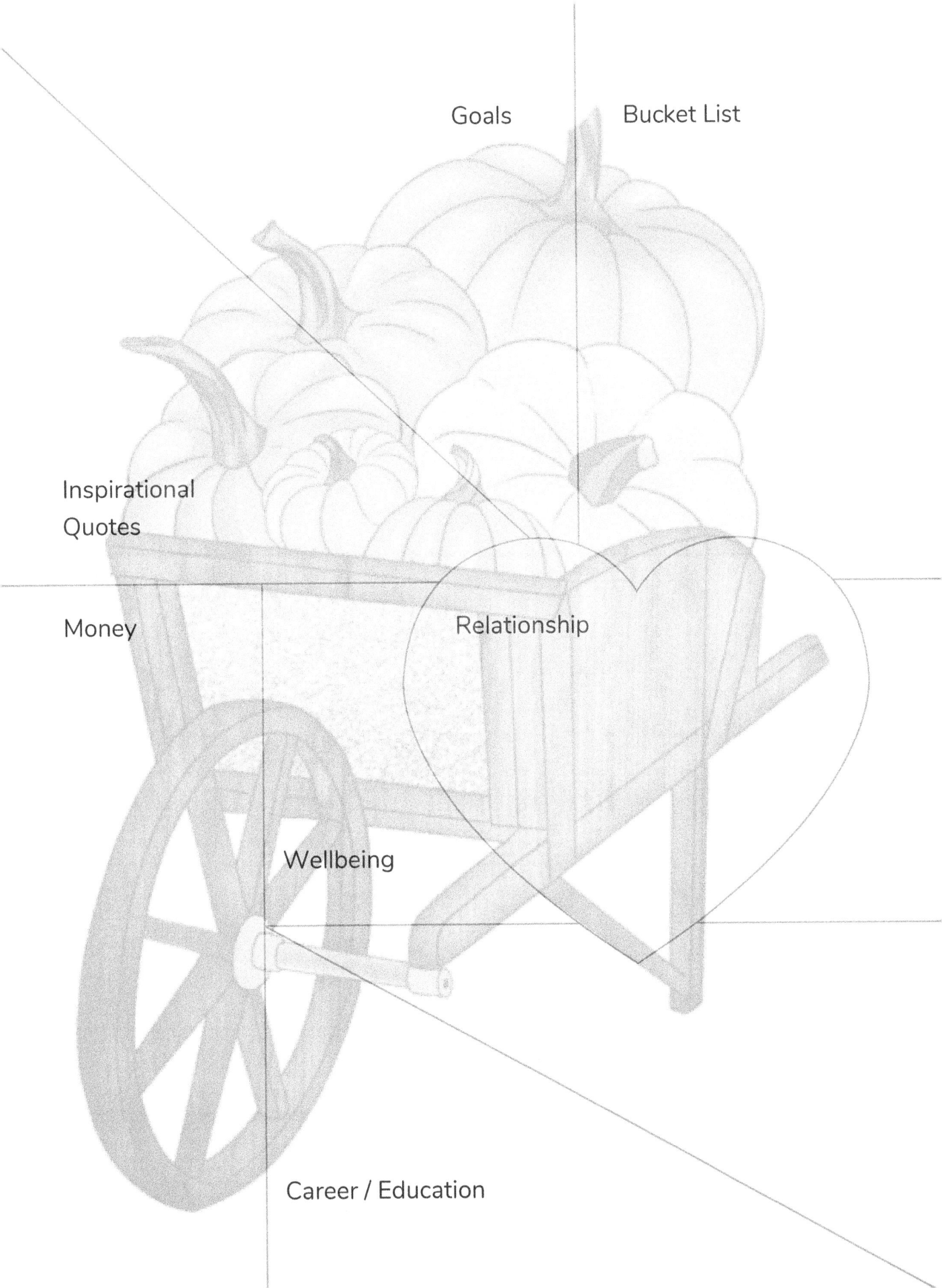

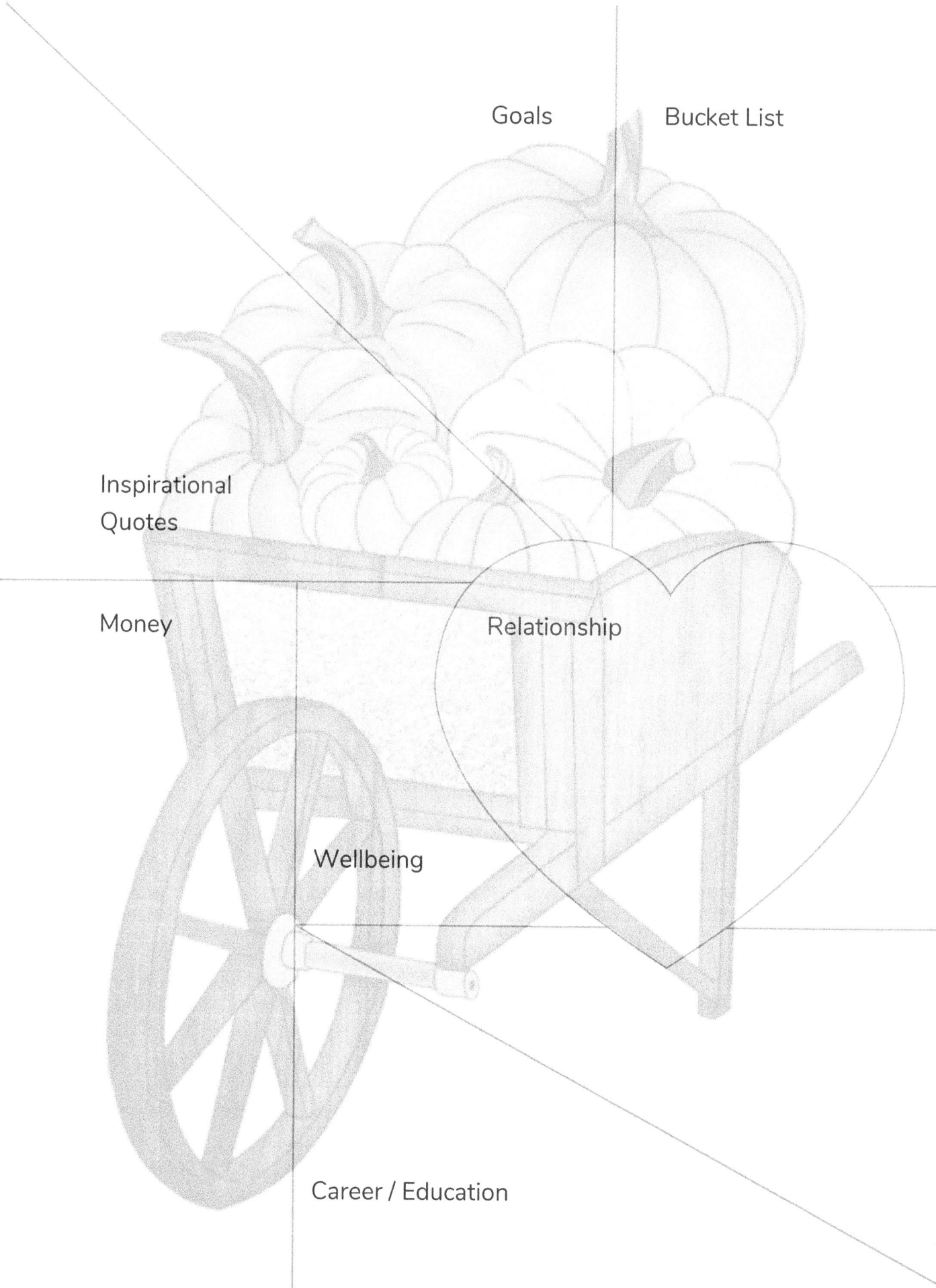

Goals

Bucket List

Inspirational Quotes

Money

Relationship

Wellbeing

Career / Education

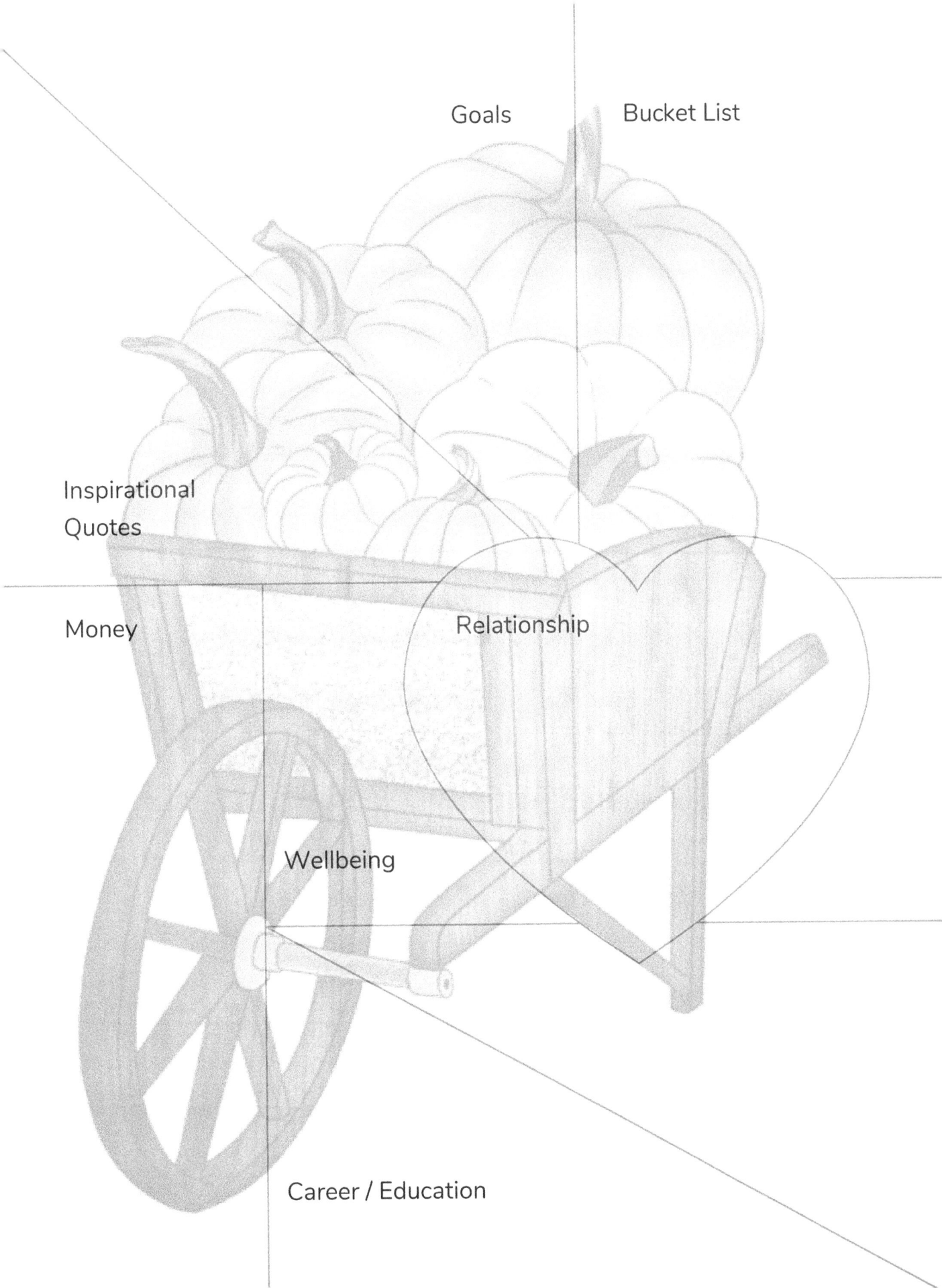

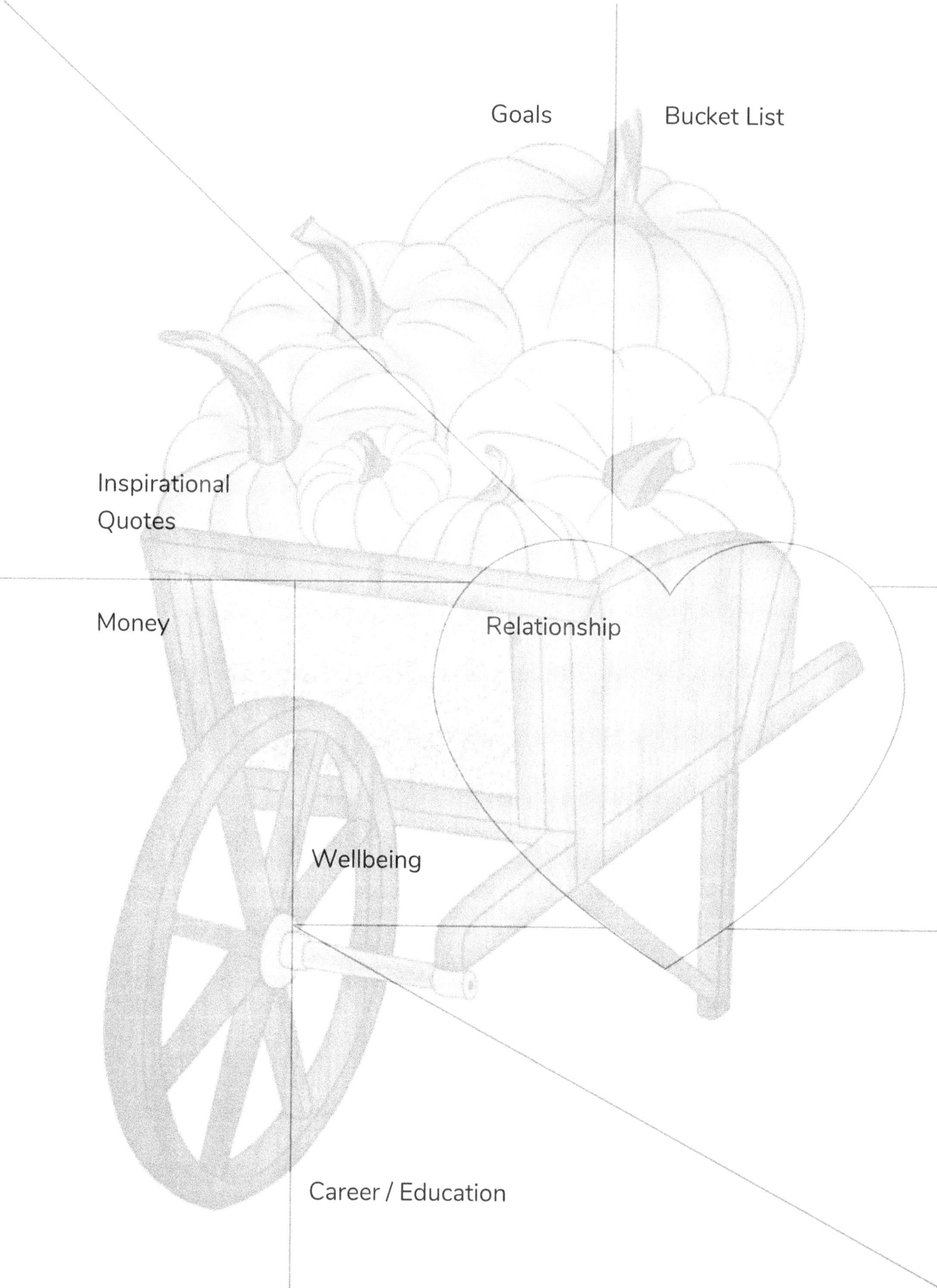

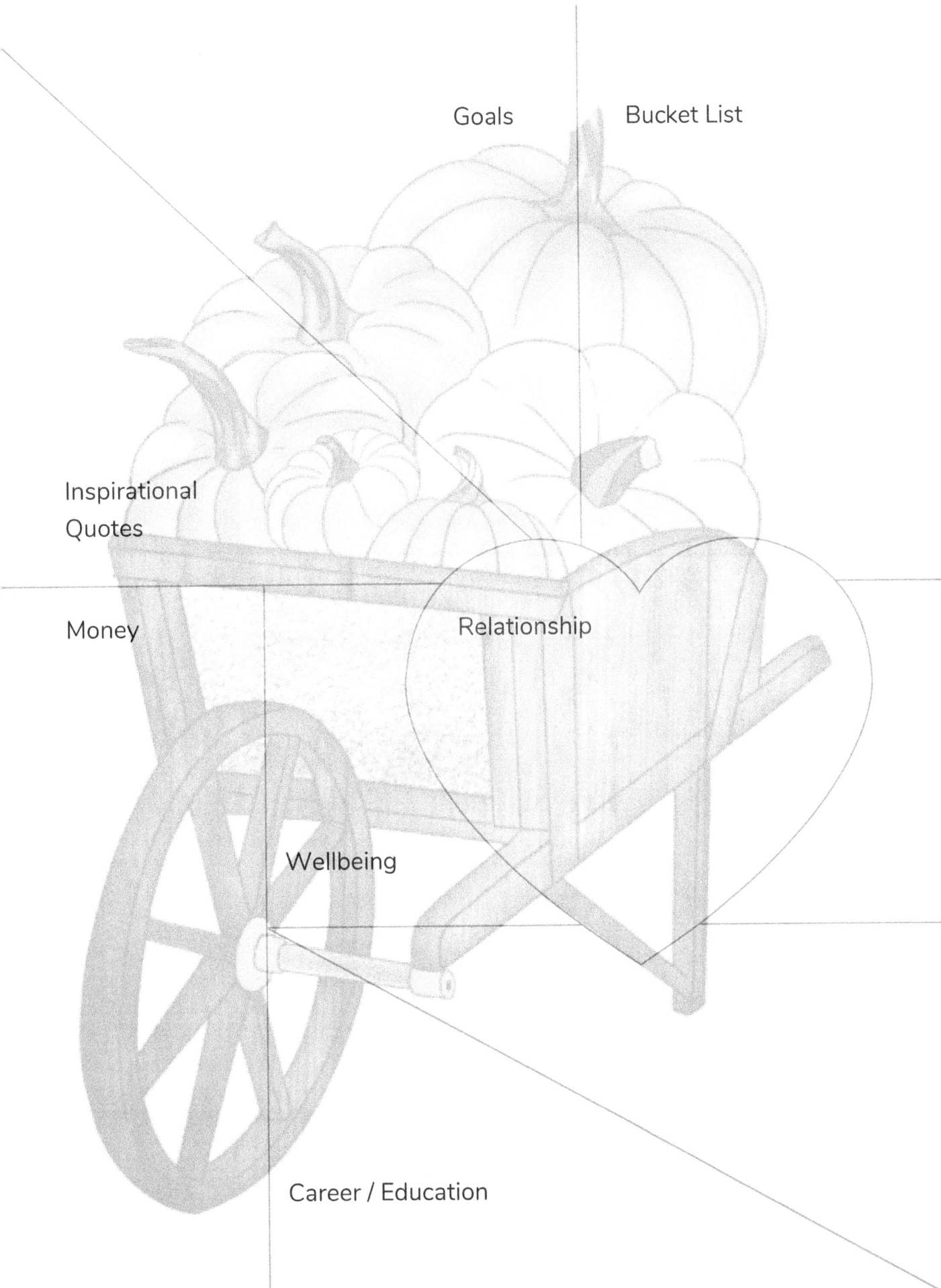

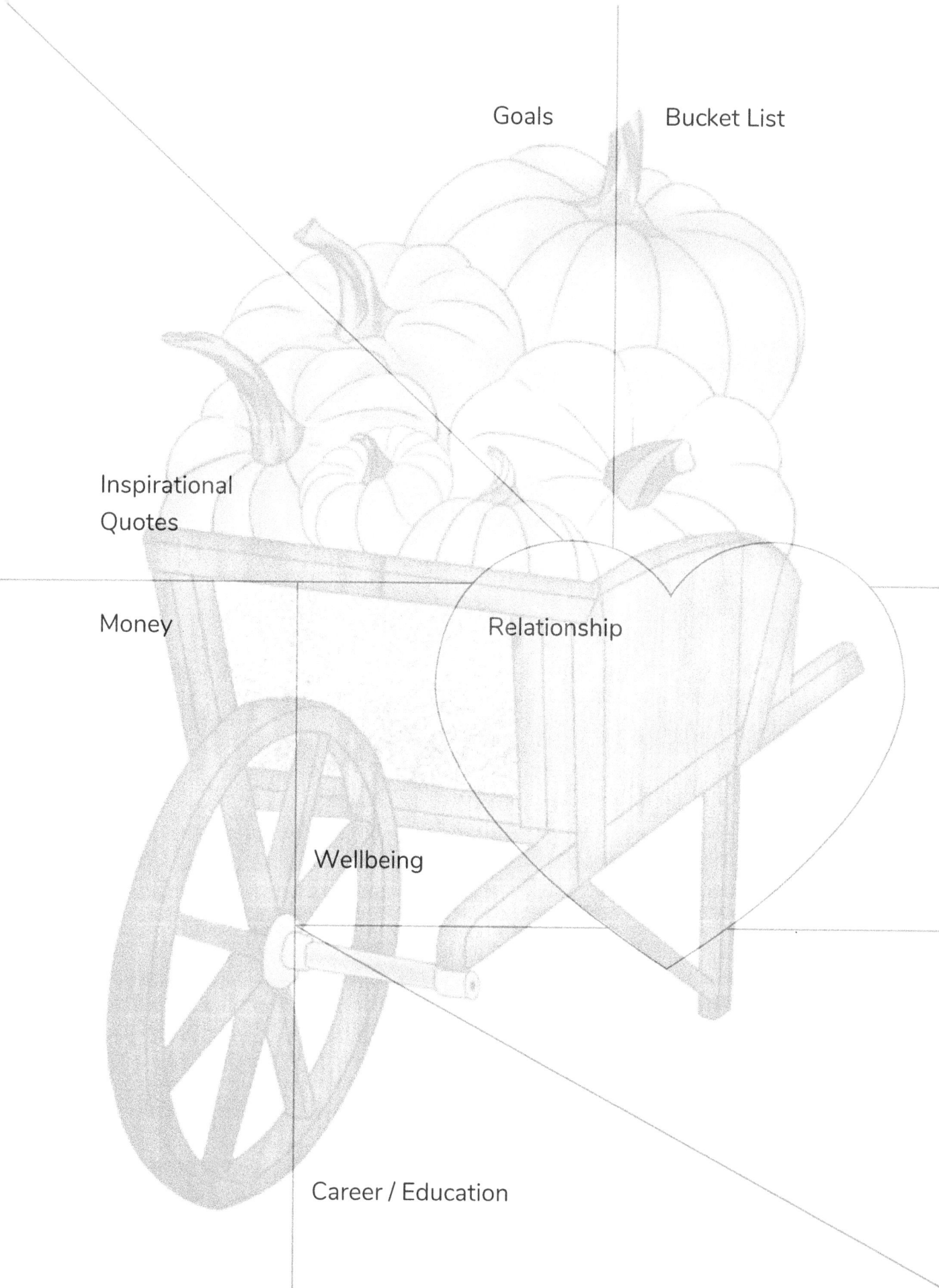

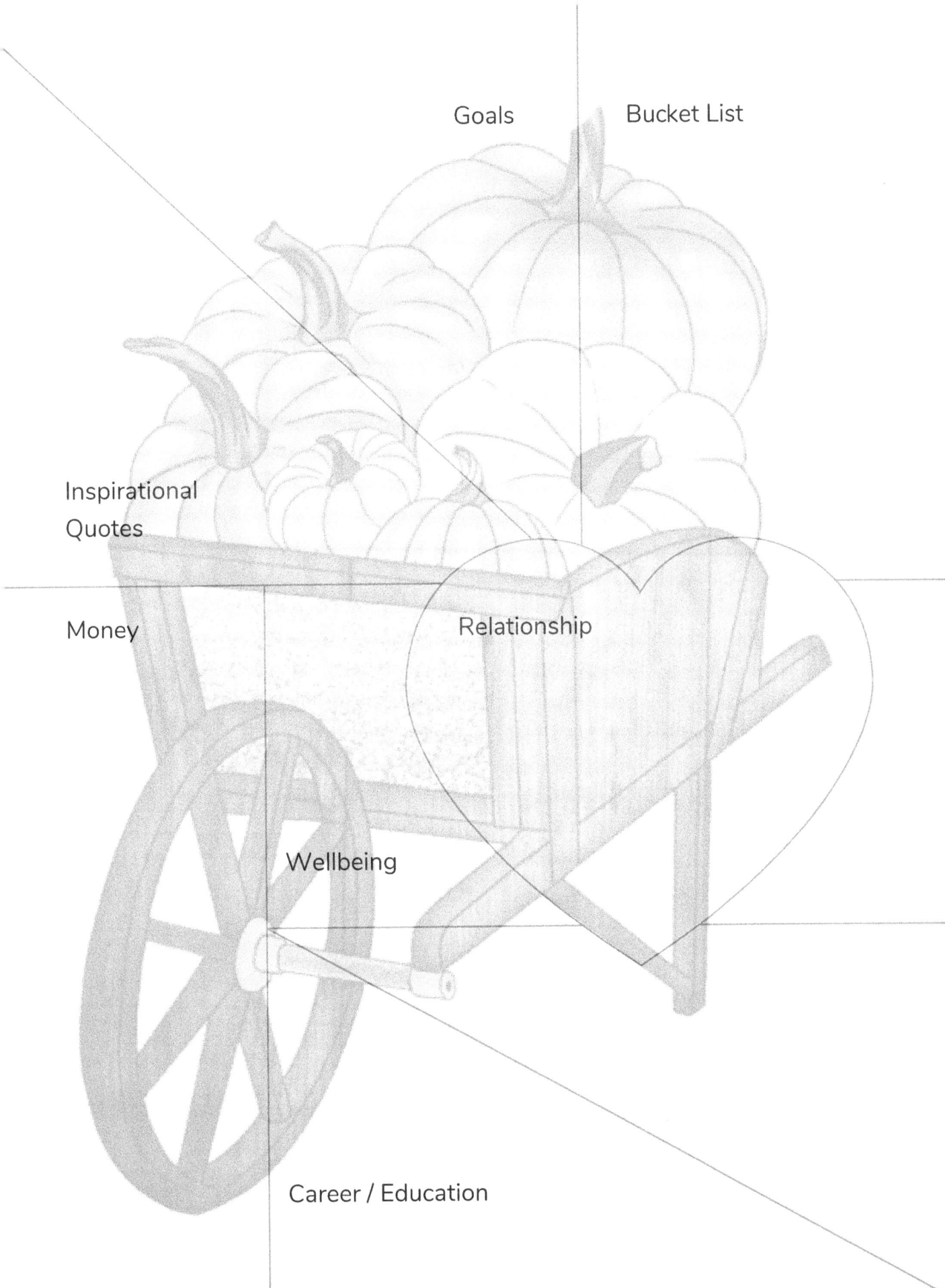

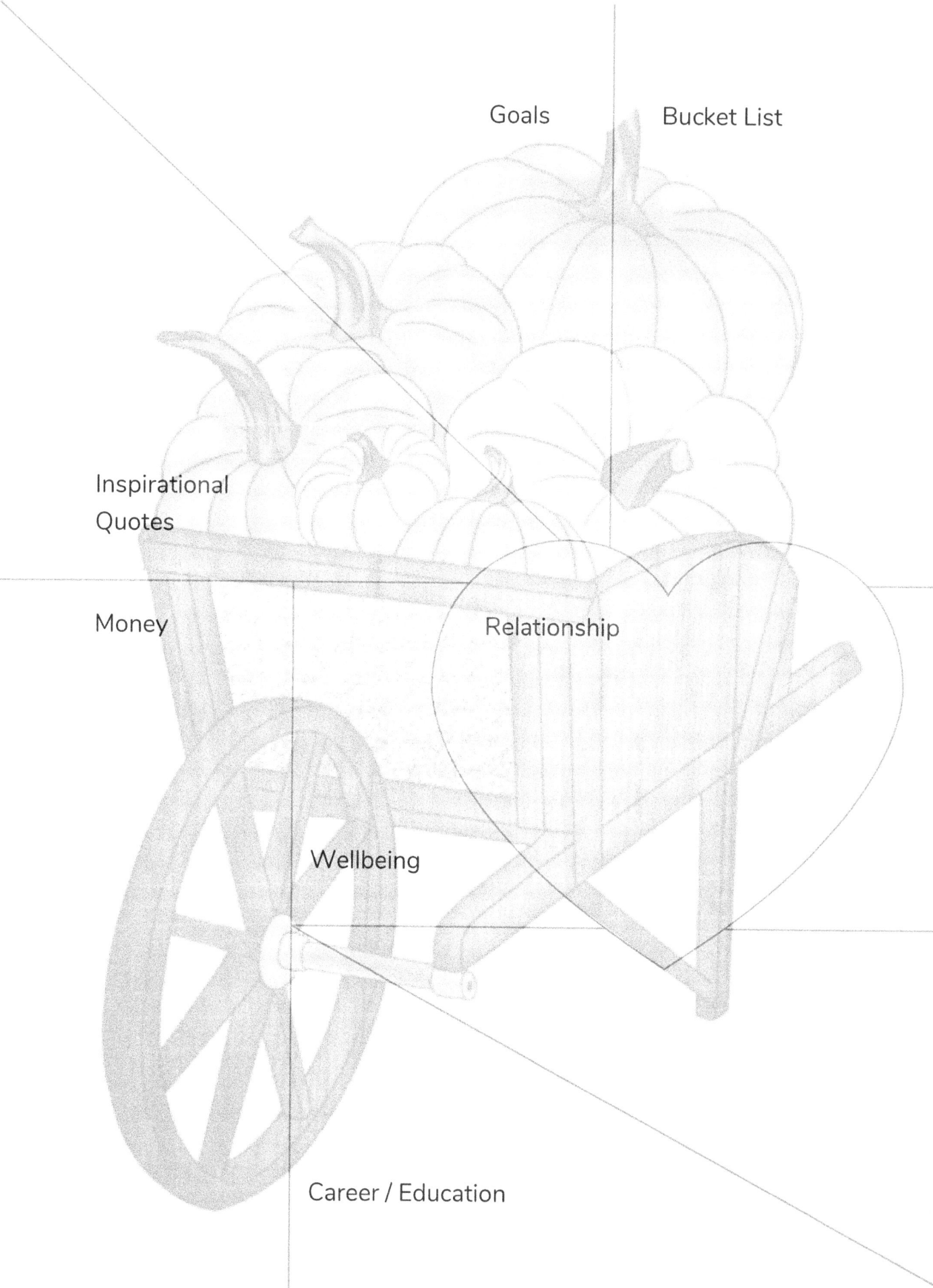

Goals Bucket List

Inspirational Quotes

Money Relationship

Wellbeing

Career / Education

November 2020

Sunday	Monday	Tuesday	Wednesday	Thursday	Friday	Saturday
1	2	3	4	5	6	7
8	9	10	11	12	13	14
15	16	17	18	19	20	21
22	23	24	25	26	27	28
29	30	1	2	3	4	5

December 2020

Sunday	Monday	Tuesday	Wednesday	Thursday	Friday	Saturday
29	30	1	2	3	4	5
6	7	8	9	10	11	12
13	14	15	16	17	18	19
20	21	22	23	24	25	26
27	28	29	30	31	1	2

Monthly Planner

Month: _____ **Year:** _____

Monday	Tuesday	Wednesday	Thursday	Friday	Saturday	Sunday
☐	☐	☐	☐	☐	☐	☐
☐	☐	☐	☐	☐	☐	☐
☐	☐	☐	☐	☐	☐	☐
☐	☐	☐	☐	☐	☐	☐
☐	☐	☐	☐	☐	☐	☐

Notes:

Monthly Planner

Month: _____ **Year:** _____

Monday	Tuesday	Wednesday	Thursday	Friday	Saturday	Sunday
☐	☐	☐	☐	☐	☐	☐
☐	☐	☐	☐	☐	☐	☐
☐	☐	☐	☐	☐	☐	☐
☐	☐	☐	☐	☐	☐	☐
☐	☐	☐	☐	☐	☐	☐

Notes:

Monthly Planner

Month: _____ **Year:** _____

Monday	Tuesday	Wednesday	Thursday	Friday	Saturday	Sunday
☐	☐	☐	☐	☐	☐	☐
☐	☐	☐	☐	☐	☐	☐
☐	☐	☐	☐	☐	☐	☐
☐	☐	☐	☐	☐	☐	☐
☐	☐	☐	☐	☐	☐	☐

Notes:

Monthly Planner

Month: _____ **Year:** _____

Monday	Tuesday	Wednesday	Thursday	Friday	Saturday	Sunday
☐	☐	☐	☐	☐	☐	☐
☐	☐	☐	☐	☐	☐	☐
☐	☐	☐	☐	☐	☐	☐
☐	☐	☐	☐	☐	☐	☐
☐	☐	☐	☐	☐	☐	☐

Notes:

Monthly Planner

Month: _____ **Year:** _____

Monday	Tuesday	Wednesday	Thursday	Friday	Saturday	Sunday
☐	☐	☐	☐	☐	☐	☐
☐	☐	☐	☐	☐	☐	☐
☐	☐	☐	☐	☐	☐	☐
☐	☐	☐	☐	☐	☐	☐
☐	☐	☐	☐	☐	☐	☐

Notes:

Monthly Planner

Month: _____ **Year:** _____

Monday	Tuesday	Wednesday	Thursday	Friday	Saturday	Sunday
☐	☐	☐	☐	☐	☐	☐
☐	☐	☐	☐	☐	☐	☐
☐	☐	☐	☐	☐	☐	☐
☐	☐	☐	☐	☐	☐	☐
☐	☐	☐	☐	☐	☐	☐

Notes:

Monthly Planner

Month: _____ **Year:** _____

Monday	Tuesday	Wednesday	Thursday	Friday	Saturday	Sunday
☐	☐	☐	☐	☐	☐	☐
☐	☐	☐	☐	☐	☐	☐
☐	☐	☐	☐	☐	☐	☐
☐	☐	☐	☐	☐	☐	☐
☐	☐	☐	☐	☐	☐	☐

Notes:

Monthly Planner

Month: _____ **Year:** _____

Monday	Tuesday	Wednesday	Thursday	Friday	Saturday	Sunday
☐	☐	☐	☐	☐	☐	☐
☐	☐	☐	☐	☐	☐	☐
☐	☐	☐	☐	☐	☐	☐
☐	☐	☐	☐	☐	☐	☐
☐	☐	☐	☐	☐	☐	☐

Notes:

Monthly Planner

Month: _____ **Year:** _____

Monday	Tuesday	Wednesday	Thursday	Friday	Saturday	Sunday
☐	☐	☐	☐	☐	☐	☐
☐	☐	☐	☐	☐	☐	☐
☐	☐	☐	☐	☐	☐	☐
☐	☐	☐	☐	☐	☐	☐
☐	☐	☐	☐	☐	☐	☐

Notes:

Monthly Planner

Month: _____ **Year:** _____

Monday	Tuesday	Wednesday	Thursday	Friday	Saturday	Sunday
☐	☐	☐	☐	☐	☐	☐
☐	☐	☐	☐	☐	☐	☐
☐	☐	☐	☐	☐	☐	☐
☐	☐	☐	☐	☐	☐	☐
☐	☐	☐	☐	☐	☐	☐

Notes:

www.ingramcontent.com/pod-product-compliance
Ingram Content Group UK Ltd.
Pitfield, Milton Keynes, MK11 3LW, UK
UKHW050416240426
12048UKWH00021B/1538